PLASTIC PANIC!

BY
ROBIN TWIDDY

POLLUTED PLANET

BookLife
PUBLISHING

©2019
BookLife Publishing
King's Lynn
Norfolk, PE30 4LS

All rights reserved.
Printed in Malaysia.

A catalogue record for this
book is available from the
British Library.

ISBN: 978-1-78637-524-7

Written by:
Robin Twiddy

Edited by:
Kirsty Holmes

Designed by:
Drue Rintoul

CONTENTS

Words that look like this are explained in the glossary on page 31.

A MESSAGE FROM
THE FUTURE

SITTING IN YOUR ROOM, YOU ARE HAPPILY ENJOYING A VIDEO FROM ONE OF YOUR FAVOURITE CONTENT CREATORS, THE BIG FOZZER.

ALRIGHT GUYS: IF YOU ARE NEW TO THE CHANNEL, THEN SMASH THAT LIKE BUTTON, AND DON'T FORGET TO SUBSCRIBE. TODAY I AM GOING TO DO A VIDEO ABOUT WHY PLASTIC IS FANTASTIC! I JUST LOVE PLASTIC...

vEejit

2:25 / 5:47

PROOF, IF PROOF BE NEED BE: PLASTIC.

28,965 views

hammerleg3nd
are you on email?

dmell0r49
@hammerleg3nd you simply have to be these days

p0ptastic43
i once sold a woman a very nice dehumidifier on QVC

plasticftw123456
plastic is almost as essential as email in this day and age. where would we be without it?!

n0thingbetter2dowithmytym
first

scanieldase
i just ate two cheese and ham slices and a share bag of M&Ms in a sad car park because i don't want my girlfriend to find out i'm a secret eater #griefisliving

SUDDENLY THE BIG FOZZER'S VIDEO IS INTERRUPTED BY STATIC...

kRzY cKKKzz zZzZZ zZzZ...

Ah, finally. There you are...

My name is Terry, and I am the last human on Earth. Things have gone terribly wrong and I need your help to save the future!

I know you probably don't believe me, but I am contacting you from the future. Listen: I was the best hacker in the world. I guess now I am the only hacker in the world. Using a quantum computer and my super know-how, I figured out how to hack back in time.

You are the only person I have been able to get through to; you have to help me save the world before it is too late.

It all began with convenience; convenience and ignorance. No-one knew that plastics would last longer than the human race! I'm sending you some extra info now.

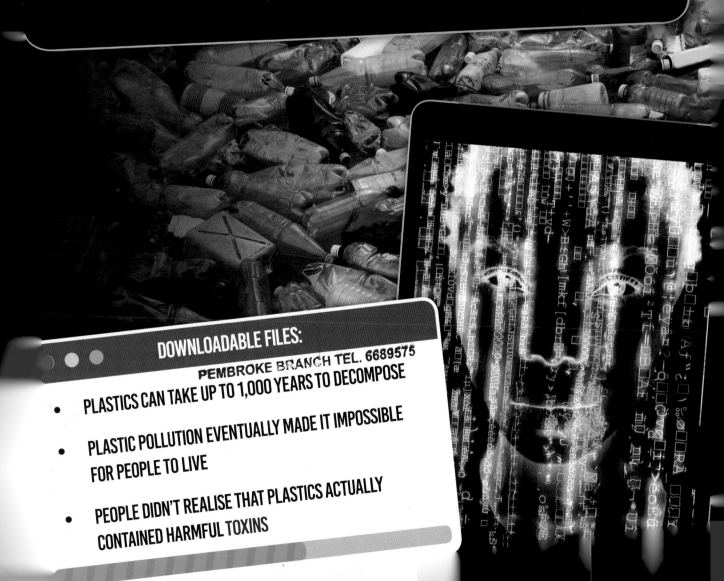

DOWNLOADABLE FILES:

PEMBROKE BRANCH TEL. 6689575

- PLASTICS CAN TAKE UP TO 1,000 YEARS TO DECOMPOSE

- PLASTIC POLLUTION EVENTUALLY MADE IT IMPOSSIBLE FOR PEOPLE TO LIVE

- PEOPLE DIDN'T REALISE THAT PLASTICS ACTUALLY CONTAINED HARMFUL TOXINS

A PLASTIC PRISON

Look, I can see that you don't believe me, but it's true! I am the last human and you are the world's only hope. If you listen very carefully and do what I tell you, we might just be able to save the future.

I can see you thinking: "How did you survive, Terry?" Well, let me tell you about my plastic prison. While the plastic piled up outside and the world became uninhabitable, I stayed here in this underground bunker!

YOU TRY TO IGNORE THE MADMAN ON YOUR TABLET AND GO TO SLEEP. JUST THE THE TV IN YOUR ROOM SWITCHES ITSELF (

No, really: listen. It is VERY important that you understand the damage all this plastic has caused. I can still find DVDs, CDs and video game discs lying aroun It's been nearly 200 years since the last one was made!

It's funny, really. These plastic bottles of water and **vacuum-sealed rations** have kept me alive, even though they are part of the problem.

YOU ASK THE MYSTERIOUS STRANGER WHAT HAPPENED TO ALL THE OTHER PEOPLE.

After a while, people realised that all the plastic wasn't going anywhere and this might be the beginning of the end. That's when the panic started!

THE PROMISE OF A PLASTIC PARADISE

Let me tell you how this whole mess got started. It began with the first real plastic in 1907. This was called Bakelite. By the mid-1950s the stuff was everywhere and things were looking good.

Plastic was great! It was cheap to make and could be moulded into any shape. Companies started replacing paper packaging with plastic wrap. Toys, televisions, phones, and even furniture were all being made from the miracle material. Little did they know of the horror lurking just around the corner.

People thought that they would build a new world from plastic; a plastic paradise. And they did! They built a new world, but it was far from the promised paradise.

ugh the 70s, 80s and 90s
se of plastic increased
and more. The real problem
the increased use of plastic

for single-use products, such
as drinks bottles and plastic
packaging. Wait: I am sendin
you some more info now.

DOWNLOADABLE FILES:

OF 2018, CLOSE TO 380 MILLION TONNES OF
ASTIC WERE PRODUCED EACH YEAR

ESTIMATED 6.3 BILLION TONNES OF PLASTIC
S PRODUCED BETWEEN 1950 AND 2018

LY AROUND 9% OF THAT 6.3 BILLION HAS BEEN
CYCLED

% HAS BEEN INCINERATED

THE PRICE OF PLASTIC!

...RE GETTING A BIT FREAKED OUT BY THIS TERRY GUY ON YOUR TABLET. ...HEAD OUT FOR A WALK AROUND THE SHOPS, BUT IN FRONT OF YOU ...ALL OF TVS QUICKLY CHANGES TO A SINGLE IMAGE... TERRY!

Hey! Where are you going?! We've got work to do! I have to tell you about the horrors of plastic production. It's not just the plastic litter that's the problem, it's also how it is made.

Plastic is made from toxic chemicals such as benzene and vinyl hydrochloride; both of these chemicals are known to be causes of a disease called cancer. The **by-products** from plastic production were found to **contaminate** the air and soil. I'm going to show you what the world outside this bunker looks like now!

The air became so thick with plastic fumes that nobody could go outside without a mask! These were bad times.

DOWNLOADABLE FILES:

- MAKING ONE PLASTIC BOTTLE RELEASES 100 TIMES MORE AIR POLLUTION THAN MAKING A GLASS BOTTLE OF THE SAME SIZE

- PLASTIC PHOTODEGRADES; THIS MEANS THAT IT DOESN'T GET ABSORBED BY NATURE WHEN IT BREAKS DOWN, IT JUST BREAKS DOWN INTO SMALLER TOXIC BITS

You know that new plastic smell? Nice, isn't it? NOPE! That's the smell of harmful chemicals being released. DON'T SNIFF THE PLASTIC!

Plastic polluted the planet in lots of ways. Plastic litter, such as crisp packets, carrier bags, six-pack holders and single-use bottles, got into the natural environment. They filled up the oceans and the countryside, suffocating and trapping animals.

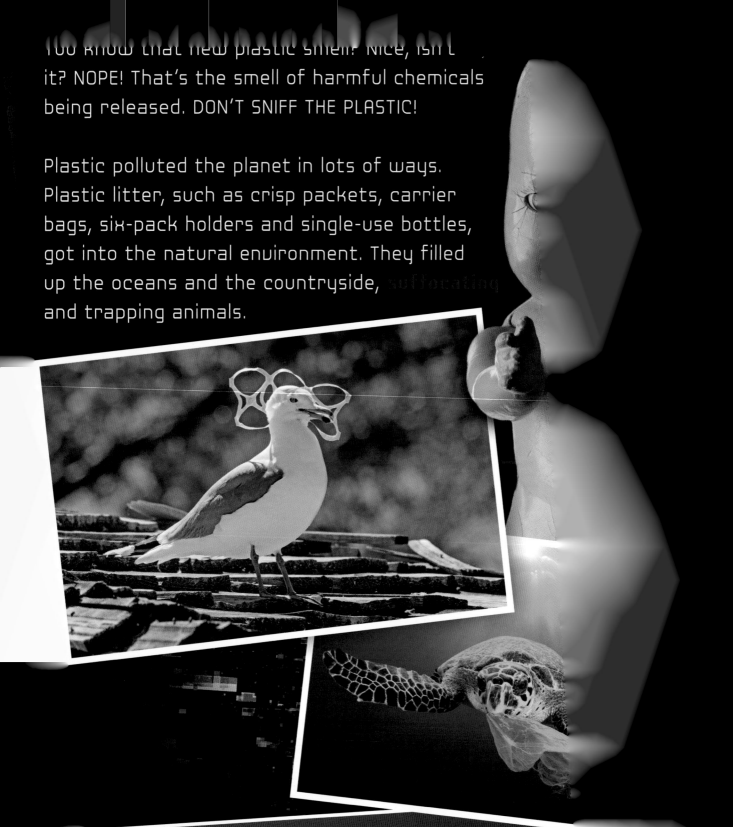

DOWNLOADABLE FILES:

CRISP PACKETS CAN TAKE BETWEEN 75–80 YEARS TO BIODEGRADE

PLASTIC DRINKS BOTTLES CAN TAKE UP TO 500 YEARS TO BREAK DOWN

PETROCHEMICAL PRODUCTS LIKE DRINKS BOTTLES NEVER FULLY BIODEGRADE – THE CHEMICALS SOAK INTO THE SOIL

Look, I know that this is upsetting, but it's important that you know what we are up against. All those chemicals started doing things to us. Fewer babies were being born each year, and more crops failed to grow properly so there was less to eat.

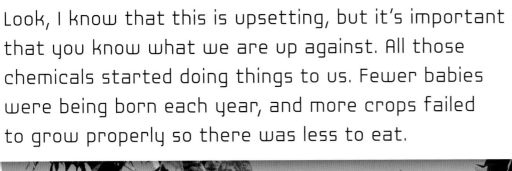

DOWNLOADABLE FILES:

- SEA TURTLES WERE DEVASTATED BY PLASTIC WASTE IN THE OCEANS

- IN 2013, 15% OF BABY SEA TURTLES WERE FOUND TO HAVE SWALLOWED ENOUGH PLASTIC TO BLOCK THEIR DIGESTIVE SYSTEMS

- MILLIONS OF MARINE BIRDS WERE KILLED EACH YEAR FROM INGESTING PLASTIC

Wildlife was particularly affected by plastic pollution. Birds and sea creatures in the oceans would often confuse plastic with food. They would swallow it and suffocate, or it would block their digestive systems and they would starve to death.

PACKAGING, PACKAGING, PACKAGING

Making just a little bit of plastic was a problem – but then people started wrapping plastic in plastic! Bonkers, right? Bags inside of bags! Multi-packs of crisps in bags, individually wrapped fruit, plastic wrapped around boxes that contain plastic-wrapped products. I'm getting dizzy just thinking about it!

Look at this banana; it comes with its own natural packaging! It doesn't need more packaging! AAAAAAAAHHHHHH! Sorry; I get a bit frustrated. But it was this kind of short-term thinking that landed me alone in this bunker!

NATURAL PROTECTIVE LAYER

OBJECT-01

OBJECT-02

[MD-34]

08953 08953
15679 15679
96842 96842

08953 08953
15679 15679
96842 96842

08953 08953
15679 15679
96842 96842

08953 08953
15679 15679
96842 96842

08953 08953
15679 15679
96842 96842

08953 08953
15679 15679
96842 96842

Group-A
22x

Group-C
18x

in 2014 was wrapped in plastic. People thought that it would make the food last longer and reduce food waste. It didn't!

Between 2004 and 2014, the amount of plastic packaging on food doubled, and so did the amount of food waste. A lot of packaging waste was made with metallised plastic. This looks a bit like tin foil, except that it can't be recycled. If you aren't sure if something is metallised, give it a scrunch. If the wrapper springs back into shape it is metallised plastic. It made food last longer, but it was not recyclable... Who thought of that?

DOWNLOADABLE FILES:

- SUPERMARKETS IN THE UK IN 2018 WERE CREATING 800,000 TONNES OF PLASTIC PACKAGING WASTE A YEAR

- EVERY SEVEN WEEKS, THE AVERAGE UK CITIZEN THROWS AWAY THEIR BODY WEIGHT IN WASTE

- 40% OF PLASTIC MADE IS USED IN PACKAGING

MOUNT NAPPY

In my time, there is a landmark we call Mount Nappy. It's exactly what it sounds like: a mountain made of nappies. I tried to climb it once; I wouldn't recommend it!

Nappies were a real problem. Not only did they take a long time to degrade, but when they did, they let out toxins that found their way into the environment. I am going to send you some more files about nappies.

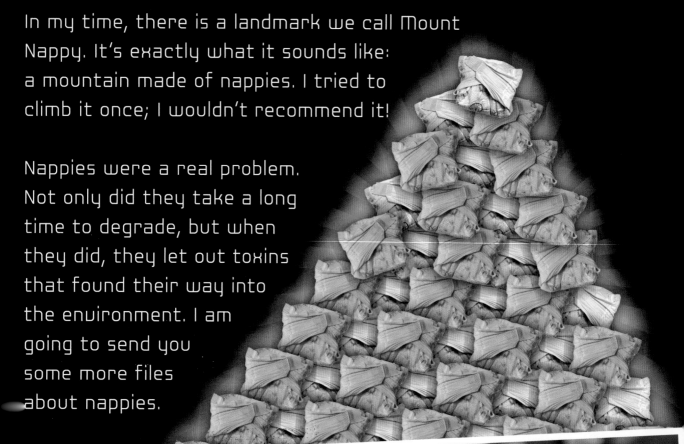

DOWNLOADABLE FILES:

- THE AVERAGE BABY USED 4–5 NAPPIES A DAY

- IN 2018, THE UK DISPOSED OF AROUND 8 MILLION NAPPIES A DAY

- DISPOSABLE NAPPIES TAKE AROUND 500 YEARS TO BIODEGRADE

en with a gas mask
s hard to breathe
t there, but I thought
at it was important to
ow you Mount Nappy.
stead of using disposable
appies, some people used
eusable cloth nappies.
only more people did!

hese nappies could be washed and were biodegradable.
though they did have some plastic in them, they were used
ver and over. There aren't any of these in Mount Nappy!

THE PLASTIC OCEAN

Have I told you about the seas? The seas have filled up with plastic! In fact, they contain more plastic than fish now. The fish that are left are all really chewy. It got so bad you could walk from Dover, in England, to Dunkirk, in France!

Since the fish couldn't be eaten anymore, all the seagulls disappeared. People couldn't travel by boat either, and I had to give up surfing! It didn't take very long before someone had set fire to the whole south Pacific Ocean!

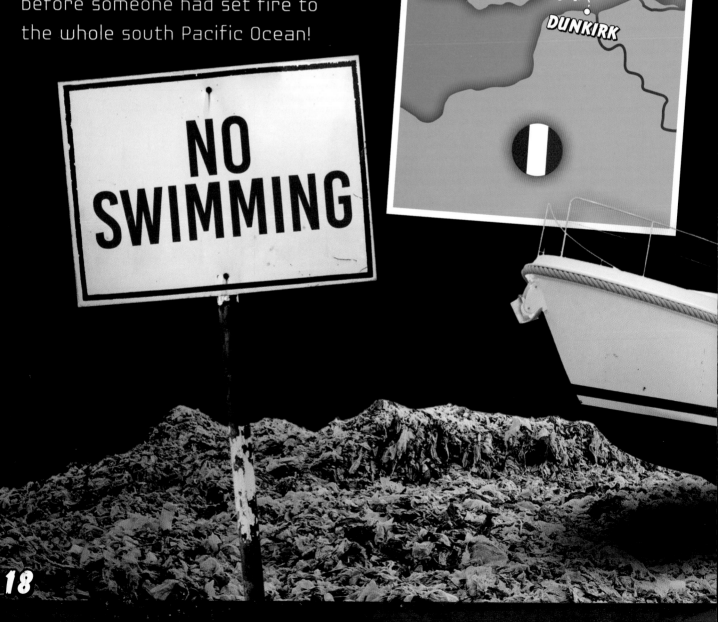

NO SWIMMING

DOVER

DUNKIRK

It happened before anyone realised. It wasn't just one thing, but rather a combination of bad choices and short-sighted decisions. Litter from urban areas, carelessly dropped, was blown into the ocean. The fishing boats threw away   nets, which then became tangled or torn. And worst of all were the companies and countries dumping waste straight into the ocean.

The Great Pacific Garbage Patch should have been an early warning. This is a patch of plastic and water that was only noticed when it became the size of Texas. Between 2000 and 2020 it became obvious that the seas were filling up with plastic, but we just kept on making and dumping the stuff until the ocean was full. I'm going to send you some more info.

DOWNLOADABLE FILES:

- SCIENTISTS PREDICTED THAT BY 2050 THERE WOULD BE AS MUCH PLASTIC IN THE OCEAN AS FISH

- 100,000 MARINE ANIMALS DIED EVERY YEAR FROM BECOMING TANGLED IN PLASTIC

- CLOSE TO 200 PIECES OF PLASTIC HAVE BEEN FOUND UNDIGESTED IN A SINGLE SEABIRD

MICRO-PLASTICS, MASSIVE PROBLEM

OK, so the biggest problem is probably the smallest one: micro-pla
Micro-plastics are tiny pieces of plastic. Sometimes they were ma
that way, and sometimes they were just broken down from bigge
plastic pollution.

For a while, companies
were adding micro-plastics
to all sorts of products,
such as shampoos, face-
creams, toothpaste and
even clothes. Why did you
people rub plastic in your
hair? Were you all mad?!

People didn't even realise that it was a problem until they started finding plastic in the fish and the birds. Then they started finding it in people. In 2018, 94% of tap water in the United States of America was contaminated with small amounts of plastic fibres.

AT THIS POINT, TERRY SEEMED TO BECOME PARTICULARLY STRANGE, SHOUTING SOMETHING ABOUT...

PLASTIC PEOPLE. PLASTIC PEOPLE! They only come at night... I've seen them. I guess they used to be like me, but they are plastic people now!

Even washing your clothes made things worse. Each wash cycle would flush up to 700,000 tiny plastic fibres into the ocean. That's why we all stopped washing our clothes. I haven't ever washed mine.

TOXIC SOLUTIONS

So the people of your time had to ask themselves a question: what to do with plastic if it won't just break down and disappear? At first, a lot of plastic went to landfill.

This wasn't a good solution; it just caused more problems. A lot of plastic waste was blown by the wind or carried by water from landfills out to sea or into the countryside. Even the plastic that did break down leached harmful chemicals into the soil and groundwater.

People did try to solve the plastic problem. They tried really hard! But there were problems with some of the ways they tried to fix it. Recycling helped – if you can't get rid of the plastic maybe you can turn it into something else...

...ven recycling caused some ...pected problems. To recycle ...ic, people needed to melt it ...n to reshape it. This released ...tile organic compounds (VOC) ...mes that are harmful to plant ...animal life. Beyond that, people ...ame very confused about what ...ld and couldn't be recycled. ...ck out these downloadable ...s to see what I mean.

DOWNLOADABLE FILES:

NON-RECYCLABLES PEOPLE TRIED TO RECYCLE

- PLASTIC BAGS
- COFFEE CUPS
- SOFT PLASTIC/LAMINATED FOIL PACKAGING
- HAND SOAP PUMP DISPENSER TOPS
- STRAWS
- CRISP PACKETS
- SHAMPOO BOTTLES AND FOOD CONTAINERS THAT HAVE NOT BEEN RINSED

Recycle, Reuse, Reduce...
AND SURVIVE

Right, the future I have shown you is pretty scary – you could say it's Terry-fying – but YOU can save it! Here is where to start.

RECYCLE

I know that I said recycling wasn't perfect but it's better than just letting that plastic float around the sea. Make sure that you and everyone you know recycles everything you can. I taught all my friends to recycle... back when I still had friends.

REUSE

Stop! Don't throw away that bottle, don't even recycle it – reuse it! That would make a perfectly good pen pot. Use it to store things around the house. Make sure you don't keep drinks inside old bottles as they

Probably the most important thing you can do is reduce the amount of plastic you use. Do I need this rubber duckie? Hmmmm... I do love him; but no, I don't need him. Look for alternatives. That means choosing to do things like using metal or glass straws instead of plastic ones. Use canvas bags instead of plastic bags and if you want company in the bath, get a real duckie! Not that there are any ducks here in my time, of course. I miss the quacking.

These are the first steps to survival. Hang on, and I'll send you some data on the best ways to reduce your plastic use.

DOWNLOADABLE FILES:

- CARRY A REUSABLE BAG FOR SHOPPING
- AVOID SYNTHETIC CLOTHING
- USE METAL OR GLASS STRAWS INSTEAD OF PLASTIC
- CARRY A REUSABLE WATER BOTTLE
- CUT OUT ALL BOTTLED DRINKS
- AVOID CHEWING GUM (MOST OF IT IS MADE FROM PLASTIC)
- AVOID SOAPS AND CARE PRODUCTS THAT CONTAIN MICROBEADS

COMMUNITY CLEAN-UP

OK, so I know I am pinning a lot on you – you can't do it all yoursel
You are going to need some help.

IT'S TIME TO START RECRUITING

Gather up all your friends and family and start making a difference. Organise a litter pick, talk to your school about going plastic-free, and educate yourself and your friends about single-use plastics. Start small. Small things grow into big things. If you can start to make a difference in your community maybe others will follow your example.

RECYCLE,
REUSE,
REDUCE

Others from your time are doing this. Trash Girl (also known as Nadia Sparkes) from Norwich, England, inspired her community and made a big impact by picking up litter near her home and putting it safely in the bin or recycling it. Be like Nadia and put the planet first!

Use social media to get the message out. Show everybody what you and others are doing. By just picking up litter on her way to school each day, Nadia became an internet sensation and brought awareness about recycling to lots of people.

Does your community have recycling bins? Talk to someone in your local council about starting a recycling campaign. Talk to local business owners about how to reduce their plastic use.

SAVE THE PLANET, SAVE YOUR BUSINESS

FRANKIE SAYS RECYCLE

RECYCLE NOW

You are doing great; I can already see some of the plastic waste disappearing. Keep it up!

STOP THE PLASTIC,
SAVE THE PLANET

This isn't going to be an easy job, but don't worry – you are not alone. There are lots of people in your time who have stopped using single-use plastic. And there are lots of companies trying to go plastic free. Asda supermarket in the UK was one of the first supermarkets to stop using single-use plastics on their own branded products.

Remember: it is about changing people's attitudes. Not that long before your time, people didn't even have plastic and there was no such thing as a single-use product.

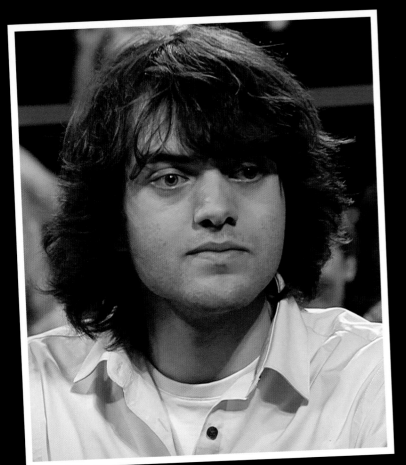

Boyan Slat is a young man from your time. He built a device that cleaned plastics up from the ocean by using the ocean's own currents to feed the plastic into anchored nets. This was a great start but, on its own, it wasn't enough. You need to support more projects like this and make sure that people know about them.

help people remember how to reuse everything. Trust me; you live in a beautiful world and it is not too late to save it. It's been a while since I have seen a real person, but if I remember correctly they are pretty reasonable things. If you can just show them the error of their ways I am sure that they will be happy to follow your lead.

everybody stops buying unnecessary plastic, companies will soon stop making it.

Now get to work. I'm counting on you!

THE FUTURE

IT MAY HAVE TAKEN EVERYTHING THAT TERRY HAD, BUT HE HAS FINALLY GOTTEN THROUGH TO YOU. YOU BEGIN TO SORT YOUR RECYCLING, REDUCE YOUR PLASTIC USE, AND TALK TO EVERYONE YOU KNOW ABOUT THE DANGERS OF PLASTICS.

Something's happening... It can't be... Everything is... changing? The world seems to be remaking itself around me! I guess you must have done it! You saved the world from plastic!

FOR THE FIRST TIME, YOU SEE TERRY'S TRUE FACE.

THANK YOU, THANK YOU, THANK YOU! Look at this beautiful world that you have restored for me, and all the rest of the world!

AND WITH THAT, TERRY DISAPPEARED. YOU THINK TO YOURSELF THAT SOMEWHERE IN THE FUTURE – A FUTURE WITHOUT PLASTIC – A HAPPY MAN NAMED TERRY IS FROLICKING IN THE SUN WITH HIS FELLOW HUMANS! TERRY LEFT YOU ONE FINAL DOWNLOADABLE FILE AS A PARTING GIFT.

DOWNLOADABLE FILES:

REMEMBER, EVERYBODY IS RESPONSIBLE FOR THE ENVIRONMENT. TO AVOID A FUTURE LIKE THE ONE I HAVE SHOWN YOU EVERYONE MUST KEEP WORKING TOGETHER TOWARDS THE BEST AND GREENEST FUTURE.

THANK YOU AGAIN.

TERRY: SIGNING OFF!

GLOSSARY

BILLION	one thousand million
BIODEGRADE	to be broken down by natural organisms such as bacteria
BY-PRODUCTS	the secondary and often unintentional result of production
CONTAMINATE	make something unclean by adding a poisonous or polluting substance to it
CONVENIENCE	when something is easily used, and fulfils a need without much effort
DIGESTIVE SYSTEMS	the parts of the body that work together to break food down and produce energy
FROLICKING	playful enjoyment or fun
IGNORANCE	lack of knowledge or awareness
INCINERATED	destroyed by burning
INGESTING	eating or absorbing
LANDFILL	where waste is buried
LEACHED	to draw out a chemical into a liquid
NYLON	strong, artificial material used to make plastic, cloth, yarn and many other products
QUANTUM COMPUTER	a very powerful computer that can carry out more complex calculations than a standard computer
SOLUTION	the fix for a problem
SUFFOCATING	dying from a lack of air or being unable to breathe
SYNTHETIC	something that isn't made from a natural material
TOXINS	toxic, poisonous or corrosive substances
UNINHABITABLE	nothing lives there because it is not possible to do so
VACUUM-SEALED RATIONS	sealed food that has had the air removed to preserve it

INDEX